THE
TOTALLY CRAB
COOKBOOK

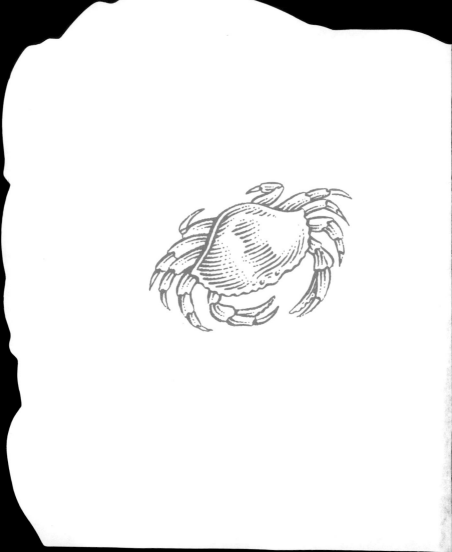

THE
TOTALLY CRAB
COOKBOOK

By Helene Siegel & Karen Gillingham

Illustrated by Carolyn Vibbert

CELESTIAL ARTS
BERKELEY, CALIFORNIA

The Totally Crab Cookbook is produced by becker&mayer!, Ltd.

Printed in Malaysia

Cover design and illustration: Dick Witt
Interior design and typesetting: Susan Hernday
Interior illustrations: Carolyn Vibbert

Library of Congress Cataloging-in-Publication Data
Siegel, Helene.
The Totally Crab Cookbook / by Helene Siegel.
    p.   cm.
ISBN-13: 978-0-89087-821-7
ISBN-10: 0-89087-821-8
1. xxx   2. xxx   II. Title.
TX749.5.B43s55   1996
641.8′4—dc20   96-35100

                                              CIP

Celestial Arts Publishing
P.O. Box 7123
Berkeley, CA 94707

Other cookbooks in this series:
The Totally Lobster Cookbook
The Totally Salmon Cookbook
The Totally Shrimp Cookbook

TO SEAFOOD LOVERS EVERYWHERE

CONTENTS

INTRODUCTION

I t takes chutzpah to cook and eat a crab.
If you are lucky enough to find one live, at a
good fish market or along the shore, the first
thing you are faced with is the elemental task of
stalking and killing your prey—one with a fierce
demeanor, ten swift legs, and legendary pincers.

Then the workout really begins. To eat the crit-
ter, you have to yank off its legs, scrape out its
entrails, crack it with a hammer, pry tight shells
open with your fingertips, and suck hard. The
optimum attire for such aerobic eating is a tarp,

or at least a plastic bib; newspapers and buckets for shells are the appropriate tabletop accessories.

As for sharing such a feast, I can tell you from experience never to order a whole crab on a first date or at a business luncheon. There is a reason the Chinese believe that courtesans do not eat crab. It is difficult, if not impossible, to appear dainty while showering your companion with shell fragments or tugging at a particularly stubborn sliver of snow-white leg meat.

For truly dedicated crab eaters, of course, these dreary details are beside the point. For them, the meat is the thing, and pulling apart a tightly packed shell is a small price to pay for such culinary gold. Such enthusiasts should turn directly to page 59, boil or steam up a mess of crabs, roll up their shirtsleeves, and dig in.

For the less industrious, we hope to spark appetites with a wide range of crabmeat delights. There are moist, tender crab cakes à la Maryland or Thailand, soft-shell crabs in sake or black bean sauce, light-as-a-feather crabmeat ravioli in tomato or soy sauce, cooked, cracked Dungeness crab in garlicky broth, Thai-spiced stir-fried noodles with crabmeat, and some of the coolest, most refreshing salads ever to grace a summer table.

As for those who prize eating over cooking when it comes to crabs, don't forget those king-sized crab legs—just waiting to be defrosted, pulled apart, and resolutely gobbled.

"Holding a glass of wine in the right hand,
Grasping a crab claw in the left hand,
And drifting along in a boat filled with wine,
Ah, my life is totally satisfied!"

        —Anonymous Chinese poem dated 256–420 A.D.

CRAB-LACED SOUPS & STARTERS

CRAB AND CORN CHOWDER

The sweetness of corn and crab is a terrific match in this easy summer soup. Large crabs can be purchased cooked, cleaned, and cracked at a good fish market.

3 tablespoons butter
1 large onion, chopped
2 garlic cloves, minced
5 ears corn, husked
salt and freshly ground pepper to taste
2 cups fish stock
2 cups half-and-half
1 jalapeño, seeded and diced
1 cooked Dungeness crab
oyster crackers *or* saltines for garnish

Melt the butter in a large stockpot over medium heat. Sauté the onion and garlic until they begin to soften, about 5 minutes. Add the kernels of 3 ears of corn. Cook 8 minutes, stirring occasionally. Transfer mixture to food processor and purée until a chunky paste is formed. Return to pot.

Add salt and pepper, fish stock, half-and-half, and jalapeño to pot and bring to a boil.

Meanwhile, crack the crab's body into 4 parts, and separate and crack the claws. Pick remaining meat from the shells, discarding the shells. Cut the remaining 2 ears of corn into 1-inch slices. Add crab and corn to soup pot, reduce to a simmer, and cook 5 minutes. Ladle into bowls and serve with oyster crackers.

SERVES 4 AS STARTER, 2 AS MAIN COURSE

CIOPPINO

Here is a quick, unfussy version of the great tomato-based fish stew from San Francisco.

2 quarts fish, chicken, *or* vegetable stock
1 (28-ounce) can Italian tomatoes
4 garlic cloves (or more), chopped
2 tablespoons chopped fresh Italian parsley
2 tablespoons chopped fresh basil
2 teaspoons chopped fresh oregano
red pepper flakes to taste
16 clams
16 mussels
1 (2½-pound) cooked crab, cracked, cleaned, and cut up
salt and freshly ground pepper to taste

Combine stock, tomatoes, garlic, parsley, basil, oregano, and red pepper flakes in a large heavy pot. Bring to a boil. Add clams and return to boil. Add mussels; cover, reduce heat, and simmer until clams and mussels open, about 5 minutes, discarding any that remain closed. Add crab and simmer 2 to 3 minutes longer, or until heated through. Season with salt and pepper.

SERVES 8

Prepicked Crabmeat
"Picked" crabmeat is meat that has been removed from the shell. Most of the crabmeat on the market is from blue crabs, although on the West Coast, fresh, picked Dungeness meat is available at better markets. Blue crabmeat is graded according to its location on the crab: jumbo or lump is large, whole pieces from the body; lump or backfin is a combination of smaller chunks and flaked white meat from the body; and claw meat is browner meat from the claws. Most of it is sold pasteurized and frozen; it can be stored in the freezer for up to three months, and in the refrigerator for about three days, with some loss of flavor each day. Blue crabmeat is the best choice for crab cakes and other traditional East Coast dishes.

CRAB AND SNOW PEA SOUP

This quick Asian soup is light and special enough to begin an elegant dinner party.

1 quart chicken stock
2 (¼-inch) slices ginger
2 garlic cloves, crushed and peeled
4 ounces snow peas, trimmed and julienned
1 egg, beaten
1 tablespoon cornstarch mixed with
    1 tablespoon water
½ pound flaked crabmeat
1 teaspoon sesame oil
2 teaspoons dry sherry
salt and freshly ground pepper to taste

Bring the chicken stock, with the ginger and garlic added, to a boil in a large stockpot or saucepan. Add the snow peas and cook over medium-high heat 2 minutes. Reduce the heat to low and cook 5 minutes. Remove and discard the garlic and ginger.

Add the egg in a slow, steady stream, stirring continuously to break into threads. Then stir in the cornstarch mixture and remove from heat. Stir in the crabmeat and remaining ingredients. Cook just to heat through and serve hot.

SERVES 4

To Purchase Live Crabs

As with all seafood, the key to good quality is purchasing from a reputable market that does a brisk business. (It is worth finding a local Asian market for fresh shellfish, since the prices will probably be much better.) Look for crabs that are lively and kicking and whose shells are not cracked. At home, store them in the bag they came in, in the refrigerator, as long as a day.

SHE-CRAB SOUP

This luxuriously thick broth was a 19th-century specialty of Savannah, Georgia, and Charleston, South Carolina. It was traditionally prepared using the prized female blue crabs and their roe. (A crab's sex can be determined by looking at the soft underside. A long, pointy apron means it is a male; a wide apron denotes a female.)

4 tablespoons butter (2 softened)
2 carrots, peeled and chopped
1 celery rib, chopped
1 medium onion, chopped
⅛ teaspoon cayenne
⅛ teaspoon crushed saffron (optional)
salt and freshly ground pepper to taste
2 cups fish stock
1 cup half-and-half
2 tablespoons all-purpose flour
½ to 1 pound blue crabmeat, in lumps
1 tablespoon cognac

½ teaspoon Worcestershire sauce
sliced fresh chives *or* garlic croutons for garnish
   (optional)

Melt 2 tablespoons of the butter in a large heavy saucepan over medium heat. Add the carrots, celery, onion, cayenne, saffron, salt, and pepper, and cook until softened, 15 minutes. Pour in the fish stock. Bring to a boil, reduce to a simmer, and cook 10 minutes. Transfer to a food processor and purée until smooth. Pour back into the pot.

Stir in the half-and-half and bring to a boil. Reduce the heat. Meanwhile, in a small bowl, knead together the softened butter and flour to make a paste. Place this paste on the end of a whisk, and whisk into the soup to thicken. Stir in remaining ingredients. Cook just to heat through and garnish, if desired, with chives or croutons.

SERVES 4

CRAB QUESADILLAS WITH MANGO SALSA

Sweet, spicy mango salsa is also terrific on grilled fish or chicken.

¼ pound flaked crabmeat
1½ tablespoons chopped fresh cilantro
½ jalapeño, seeded and minced
safflower or vegetable oil for coating
4 flour tortillas, taco size
2 cups shredded Monterey Jack cheese

MANGO SALSA

1 mango, peeled, seeded, and diced
1 tablespoon lemon *or* lime juice
½-inch length ginger, peeled and grated
2 tablespoons chopped red onion
pinch cayenne pepper

To make salsa, mix together all the ingredients and chill.

In a small bowl, mix together crabmeat, cilantro, and jalapeño.

Heat a 10-inch cast-iron skillet over medium heat and lightly coat with oil. Place 1 tortilla in the pan, cook less than a minute, and turn. Scatter on 1 cup of the cheese. Top with an even layer of half the crab mixture, and top with another tortilla. Press with spatula, reduce heat to medium-low, and cook until the cheese is melted and the tortillas are charred in spots, about 5 minutes total, turning frequently with a spatula. Transfer to a platter and repeat. To serve, slice each into quarters and top with salsa.

SERVES 4

CRAB AND SCALLION FRITTATA

Eggs and crabmeat, with their delicate taste and texture, are a delightful combination.

6 eggs
8 scallions, white and green, chopped
½ pound flaked crabmeat
¼ cup half-and-half
2 dashes Tabasco
salt and freshly ground pepper to taste
2 tablespoons butter
¼ cup grated Parmesan cheese (optional)

Beat the eggs in a large bowl. Add the scallions, crabmeat, half-and-half, Tabasco, salt, and pepper, and gently mix.

Melt the butter in a large nonstick ovenproof skillet over medium-high heat. Pour in the egg mixture, swirl to evenly distribute, and reduce the heat to medium-low. Cook until edges are set and top is slightly liquid.

Turn on the broiler.

Sprinkle the Parmesan cheese over the top and place under the broiler. Cook less than a minute, just to set, and remove. Cool slightly and cut into wedges to serve hot or at room temperature.

SERVES 6

JAPANESE CRAB CUPS

In this easy version of sushi, sweet sticky rice and crab are molded into small cups.

1 cup short-grain rice, well rinsed
1¼ cups water
3 tablespoons rice vinegar
2 teaspoons sugar
½ teaspoon salt
½ pound flaked *or* shredded crabmeat
1 kirby cucumber, peeled and thinly sliced
2 tablespoons sesame seeds, toasted
soy sauce for drizzling

Bring the water, with 1 tablespoon of the vinegar added, to a boil in a small pot. Add the rice, stir, and cover the pot. Cook over low heat 15 minutes. Remove from heat and let sit, covered, 10 minutes.

In a small bowl, combine the remaining vinegar, sugar, and salt. Empty the rice onto a baking tray and spread thinly with a wooden spoon dipped in water. Then slowly drizzle on the vinegar mixture, stirring and tossing to mix and cool.

Spread the crab in an even layer on the bottom of six ½-cup ramekins. Top each with a thin layer of cucumber. Layer a portion of rice evenly on top, pressing and leveling the top with moist fingertips. Cover with plastic, top with a weight (a small glass or cup is fine), and let sit 30 minutes at room temperature, or up to three hours in the refrigerator.

Run a knife along the edges to loosen, and invert each onto a plate. Sprinkle the tops with sesame seeds and serve with soy sauce for drizzling.

SERVES 6

CRAB SPRING ROLLS

Frozen phyllo sheets, available in the supermarket's frozen baking section, are a good substitute for the more authentic Vietnamese wrappers. If you can find the real thing, these salad-filled rolls need not be cooked.

6 ounces flaked crabmeat
3 scallions, white and green, cut in 2-inch
    lengths and shredded
½ medium jicama, peeled and shredded
1 large carrot, peeled and shredded
1 teaspoon minced garlic
10 mint leaves, chopped
2 teaspoons Thai fish sauce *or* soy sauce
½ teaspoon sugar
freshly ground pepper to taste
10 phyllo sheets, thawed
¼ cup peanut *or* vegetable oil, warmed

Preheat the oven to 375 degrees F.

Combine all of the ingredients, except the phyllo and oil, in a large bowl. Cover the phyllo sheets with a damp towel. On a table or work counter, arrange the bowl of filling, the covered phyllo sheets, and the warm oil.

Lay each sheet, one at a time, on your work surface and lightly coat with oil. Place about ½ cup of filling in a rectangle in the center of the bottom third of the sheet, leaving 2 inches bare on either side. Fold over the sides to cover, and fold up the bottom flap. Continue rolling to form a plump cylinder. Brush the final edge with oil and press to seal. Place the rolls in a baking pan. Bake 20 to 25 minutes, until barely golden. Cool slightly and serve with spicy dipping sauce.

SERVES 6

FRIED CRAB WONTONS

These deep-fried tidbits are a sure cocktail party hit.
You can combine soy sauce, rice vinegar, and scallions
for a good, quick dipping sauce.

½ pound flaked crabmeat
½ cup minced scallions
1½ teaspoons minced garlic
salt and freshly ground pepper to taste
about 20 wonton skins
vegetable oil for frying

In a bowl, combine the crab, scallions, garlic, salt, and pepper.

Working on a counter with a cup of cold water nearby, top each wonton skin, one at time, with a scant tablespoon of filling. Spread it in a line in the center and roll into a tight little cylinder. Seal the final edge by moistening the tip with water and pressing closed. Moisten, twist, and seal the outside edges.

Fill a large skillet to a depth of 2 inches with oil and bring to deep-fry temperature. Fry the wontons a few at a time, turning once and cooking until golden all over, about 1 minute. Remove with slotted spoon and drain on paper towels. Serve with dips.

MAKES ABOUT 18 PIECES

Like most seafood, crabmeat is high in protein, rich in minerals, and low in fat.

CALIFORNIA DEVILED-CRAB EGGS

These lovely stuffed eggs are a guaranteed hit at summer barbecues or potlucks.

6 hard-boiled eggs
¾ cup crabmeat
2 tablespoons chopped fresh chives
2 tablespoons mayonnaise
1 tablespoon rice vinegar
1 teaspoon wasabi paste
salt and freshly ground pepper to taste
¼ small avocado
sliced pickled ginger and soy sauce for garnish

Cut eggs in half. Remove yolks and set whites aside.

In bowl, combine yolks with crab, chives, mayonnaise, rice vinegar, and wasabi. Mix with fork to blend. Season with salt and pepper. Pile yolk mixture into whites, mounding high.

Cut avocado into 12 equal pieces. Top each egg half with avocado. Arrange eggs on serving dish and serve with ginger and soy sauce.

MAKES 12

The Species Crab

Crabs are a hardy crustacean. Evidence of crab life dates back 200 million years to the Jurassic period. More than 4,500 species are known to exist today living in habitats as varied as bays and oceans, under the ground, and in empty shells. Three characteristics that have helped the species prosper are its ability to run fast (it doesn't need to turn to change direction), its ability to shed a leg or claw rather than remain trapped, and its fabulous sex life (more about this later). For the American cook, there are two types of crab worth thinking about: those with meaty bodies, like Dungeness and blue, and those with long, meaty legs and claws, such as the king, snow, and stone.

CRAB CEVICHE

The sharp, fresh Latin flavors of ceviche highlight those of sweet crabmeat.

2 cups flaked crabmeat
½ cup chopped seeded tomatoes
¼ cup chopped scallions
2 to 3 tablespoons chopped fresh cilantro
1 small jalapeño *or* serrano chile, stemmed, seeded, and chopped
2 tablespoons olive oil
¼ cup freshly squeezed lime juice
salt and freshly ground pepper to taste
lettuce leaves *or* avocado slices

In a bowl, combine crabmeat, tomatoes, scallions, cilantro, chile, olive oil, and lime juice. Chill. Season with salt and pepper. Serve in individual bowls, on lettuce leaves, or on avocado slices.

SERVES 6

COOL CRABMEAT SALADS

CABBAGE CRAB SLAW

Here is an upscale slaw to serve with grilled steaks for those surf-'n-turf occasions.

1 small *or* ½ large red cabbage, shredded
½ pound flaked crabmeat
¼ cup sherry wine vinegar
1 tablespoon sugar
½ teaspoon Dijon mustard
¼ teaspoon prepared horseradish
1 teaspoon celery seed
salt and freshly ground pepper to taste
½ cup olive oil

Combine the cabbage and crabmeat in a large bowl and mix well.

In a small bowl, whisk together vinegar, sugar, mustard, horseradish, celery seed, salt, and pepper. Add oil and whisk to make a dressing. Pour over cabbage mixture and toss well to evenly coat. Store in the refrigerator for up to a day before serving.

SERVES 4 TO 6

Dungeness, or Cancer magister, is the premier Pacific coast crab. Primarily harvested in California, Oregon, and Washington, it can be found as far south as Baja California and as far north as Alaska. The commercial crab industry in this region began in 1863 in San Francisco Bay. Dungeness are large, meaty crabs, weighing in at 1½ to 4 pounds, with 25-percent meat. On the West Coast, Dungeness can be purchased live, cooked, cleaned, and cracked or frozen. In upscale markets the meat may be available picked, but if not, the large, meaty bodies and claws are relatively easy to pick. The season for Dungeness landings, or harvests, usually peaks in the winter, and price varies according to availability. For a crab feast, allow one Dungeness for each guest, since each crab yields about ½ pound of sweet, flaky meat. Boiling or steaming is the easiest way to cook live crabs, and already-cooked meat in the shell can be added to soups and quick sautés. Just be careful not to overcook the already-cooked meat.

CRAB LOUIS

This old San Francisco specialty of crisp iceberg lettuce, ice-cold crab, and Russian dressing is just right for hot summer nights. (Use the leftover dressing on turkey sandwiches.)

LOUIS DRESSING

1 cup mayonnaise
¼ cup prepared chili sauce
2 tablespoons lemon juice
1 teaspoon Worcestershire sauce
1 tablespoon sweet relish
5 scallions, white and green, chopped

1 large head iceberg lettuce, shredded
4 hard-boiled eggs, peeled and halved
2 large tomatoes, cut in wedges
4 king crab legs, thawed and picked, *or*
    1 pound picked Dungeness meat

Make the dressing by mixing all the ingredients together in a bowl. Store in the refrigerator.

Divide the lettuce into 4 portions and place a bed in each large bowl or plate. Garnish the edges with eggs and tomatoes. Mound the crabmeat in the center and spoon on dressing, or serve on the side for dipping.

SERVES 4

Surimi, otherwise known as imitation crabmeat, is a mixture of lean Pacific whitefish like pollack and whiting. Although its low cost makes it tempting, do not substitute it in cooked dishes, as it will not hold up to heat. Use it only in cold, uncooked foods such as salads or sushi, if you must use it at all.

STUFFED AVOCADO SALAD

This refreshing crab salad can also be stuffed into hollowed-out tomato halves.

6 tablespoons lime juice
1 tablespoon Dijon mustard
2 teaspoons minced garlic
½ cup olive oil
salt and freshly ground pepper to taste
¾ pound flaked crabmeat
½ cup corn kernels, blanched
3 tablespoons chopped red onion
1 serrano chile, seeded and minced
4 ripe Haas avocados, peeled, pitted, and halved

Whisk together lime juice, mustard, garlic, olive oil, salt, and pepper in a bowl to make a dressing.

In another bowl, mix together the crab, corn, onion, and serrano. Pour all but ¼ cup of dressing on crab mixture and toss well. Drizzle a tablespoon of dressing on each avocado half. Scoop the crab salad into the avocado halves (overflows are fine) and serve cold.

SERVES 4

The Sex Life of a Crab

The mating ritual of the blue crab is an example of admirable tenderness. The male stands on his toes and the female rocks from side to side to indicate readiness. He then cradles her with his claws and carries her that way for two days while she molts. The male then turns the female over so they are belly to belly, exposing her soft, new skin. They join and stay locked in their embrace for about twelve hours. Afterward, he carries her until her shell is hard enough to protect her. As soon as they unlock, she dashes off to spawn.

COLD CRAB LEGS WITH DIPS

Allow about one leg per guest and feel free to use your favorite prepared cocktail sauce, drawn butter, or the "Louis Dressing" on page 36 as a dip, in addition to the ones described here.

frozen Alaskan king crab legs, broken and split
    open, or stone crab claws, cracked
lemon wedges for garnish

Defrost crab legs or claws in the refrigerator about 6 hours or at room temperature 2 to 3 hours. Chill and serve with small forks, lemon wedges, and dips.

King crabs, also known as red, blue, brown, and Alaskan king, are prized for their fabulous long, sweet legs. The bodies are not even brought to market. The legs, however, are available cooked, cut, split, and frozen year-round, making them the most easily accessible crabmeat still in the shell. Not considered a true crab because its legs are jointed behind its body, the king is caught in the cold northern waters of the Pacific and Bering Seas,

QUICK ROUILLE

½ cup mayonnaise
1 red bell pepper, roasted, peeled, seeded,
 and chopped
2 teaspoons chopped garlic
salt, freshly ground pepper, and paprika to taste

Combine all of the ingredients in a food processor or blender, and purée until smooth. Serve or refrigerate.

MAKES ABOUT ¾ CUP

---

starting in Vancouver and extending north to Alaska and west to Russia. Kings are kept alive in tanks on fishing boats and then brought to processing plants, where they are boiled in salted water and then frozen for shipment. About 1 pound of legs contains ½ pound of meat. Allow one to two legs per guest, and have your market cut and split them. They can simply be defrosted and eaten cold or quickly heated under the broiler or grill.

PINE NUT SALSA

¾ cup pine nuts
2 hard-boiled egg yolks
2 tablespoons capers
1 cup plain yogurt
salt and freshly ground pepper to taste

Combine all of the ingredients in a blender and purée until smooth. Adjust with salt and pepper, and serve or chill.

MAKES ABOUT 1½ CUPS

Snow, or tanner and queen, crab is a large, long-legged crab found in both the Atlantic and the Pacific. Like the king, it is never brought to market live; rather, it is sold cooked and frozen as legs, claws, or flaky picked meat. In my experience, it is not as tasty as king crab, nor is it as readily available, though its meat is easily accessible.

CRAB CUCUMBER SALAD

This cool, easy salad is a nice way to begin an elegant dinner party.

1 pound Japanese cucumbers, peeled, halved
  lengthwise, seeded, and sliced
1 cup crabmeat
¼ cup rice vinegar
1 tablespoon sugar
1 teaspoon sesame oil
2 thin slices fresh ginger, minced
toasted sesame seeds for garnish

In a bowl, combine cucumber, crab, vinegar, sugar, sesame oil, and ginger. Toss to combine. Chill. Toss again before serving. Serve sprinkled with sesame seeds.

SERVES 6

WARM KING CRAB LEGS WITH LEMON VINAIGRETTE

King crab legs are a terrific summer food. Readily available in the freezer at the supermarket, they defrost quickly, and require little or no heat to prepare.

4 Alaskan king crab legs, thawed, cracked,
   and split
olive oil for brushing
2 bunches watercress, trimmed, washed, and cut
   in 2-inch lengths
6 tablespoons olive oil
6 tablespoons lemon juice
2 garlic cloves
salt and freshly ground pepper to taste

Preheat the broiler or grill.

Arrange the leg pieces in a single layer on a tray and lightly brush with olive oil. Broil or grill about 3 minutes, turning once.

Meanwhile, place the watercress in a bowl. In another bowl, whisk together the olive oil, lemon juice, garlic, salt, and pepper. Spoon about 2 tablespoons of dressing on the salad and toss. Divide and place on 4 serving plates.

When the legs are ready, drizzle the remaining dressing over the hot legs on the tray. Top each salad with warm legs and serve.

Serves 4

CRAB TOSTADITOS

This tart Mexican crab salad is a favorite nibble for cocktail parties.

½ pound flaked crabmeat
¼ cup finely chopped green Spanish olives
½ cup chopped cilantro leaves
3 tablespoons minced red onion
2 plum tomatoes, seeded and diced
2 tablespoons red wine vinegar
2 tablespoons lime *or* lemon juice
2 tablespoons olive oil
Tabasco
salt and freshly ground pepper to taste
corn tortilla chips *or* tostada shells
1 avocado, peeled and thinly sliced,
   or lettuce, for garnish

In a large bowl, mix together crabmeat, olives, cilantro, onion, and tomatoes.

In a small bowl, whisk together red wine vinegar, lime juice, and olive oil. Season to taste with Tabasco, salt, and pepper. Pour over the crab mixture and toss well. Cover and chill about 4 hours.

To serve as hors d'oeuvres, top each tortilla chip with a spoonful of crab salad and garnish with avocado. Or serve on a bed of shredded, dressed lettuce inside a crisp tostada shell.

MAKES 24 PIECES OR 4 TOSTADAS

"The stone crab is much larger than the northern crab and has a shell harder than a landlord's heart."
        —Damon Runyon

Softshell crabs are blue crabs in the molting stage. Available frozen all year round, and fresh in the late spring and summer, they are a delight for lazy crab eaters since, once they are cleaned, they are entirely edible. Softshells cost three times as much as hardshells because of the labor-intensive harvesting process. Beginning in early May, fishermen watch for the first signs of shedding when the backfins begin to turn pink. Since the shells stay soft for only a few hours, molters are quickly transferred to special boxes for observation and removed as soon as they shed. (Their shells will reharden within a few hours.) Softshells' crisp texture and delicate flavor are best highlighted by quick sautéing or frying. Allow one per appetizer and two per entrée serving.

THIN-SKINNED SOFTIES

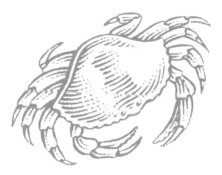

SOFTSHELL CRABS WITH HOT SAKE GINGER VINAIGRETTE

The sharpness of ginger nicely balances the richness of softshell crabs.

4 softshell crabs, cleaned and patted dry
salt and freshly ground pepper to taste
flour for dredging
2 tablespoons peanut oil
2 tablespoons butter
2 teaspoons freshly grated ginger
1 teaspoon minced garlic
2 scallions, thinly sliced
¼ cup sake

Season the crabs all over with salt and pepper. Dredge with flour and pat off excess.

Heat the oil and butter in a large skillet over medium-high heat. Sauté the crabs, backs down first, about 1½ minutes per side. Transfer to a platter.

Add the ginger, garlic, and scallions to the pan and sauté just until the aroma is released. Pour in the sake and cook a minute, scraping the bottom of the pan to release the browned bits. Season with salt and pepper, spoon over the crabs, and serve.

SERVES 2 TO 4

The Crab Body

The body of a crab is a fusion of head and thorax covered by a hard carapace, or shell. True crabs have five pairs of legs, including one ending in claws and one in backfins. Four sets are jointed toward the face. Crabs grow by shedding their shells, or molting, as many as twenty times in a lifespan of three to five years. They have excellent vision and hearing; and as for their ability to run, it is difficult to imagine a faster crustacean.

THAI PAN-FRIED CRABS

Here is another Asian take on those lovely little crustaceans—softshell crabs.

1 tablespoon Thai fish sauce *or* soy sauce
1 teaspoon brown sugar
2 serrano chiles, thinly sliced
¼ cup lime juice
4 softshell crabs, cleaned and patted dry
salt and freshly ground pepper to taste
flour for dredging
3 tablespoons butter
1 teaspoon freshly grated ginger
1 teaspoon minced garlic
½ bunch cilantro, chopped

In a small bowl, combine the fish sauce, sugar, chiles, and lime juice and set aside.

Season the crabs all over with salt and pepper. Dredge with flour and pat off excess.

Heat the butter in a large skillet over medium-high heat. Sauté the crabs, backs down first, about 1½ minutes per side. Transfer to a platter.

Add the ginger and garlic to the pan and cook less than a minute. Pour in the fish sauce mixture and cook, scraping the bottom of the pan, an additional minute. Stir in the cilantro and season with salt and pepper. Spoon sauce over the crabs and serve.

SERVES 2 TO 4

To Clean Softshells

Though it is not absolutely necessary, most of us like our softshells cleaned before cooking. (A good market will do this for you.) Pull up and discard the apron from the underside. Gently lift the top shell and scrape out the gills with a paring knife, and snip off the crab's face, eyes, and mouth with scissors.

SOFTSHELL CRAB CLUB

Here is a club sandwich to die for: a crunchy, juicy, softshell crab served on a mayo-slathered bun with crisp lettuce and a moist tomato slice.

¼ cup all-purpose flour
¼ cup cornmeal
½ teaspoon Old Bay seasoning
salt to taste
2 eggs, beaten
4 softshell crabs, cleaned and patted dry
vegetable *or* safflower oil for frying
4 kaiser or other crusty rolls, split
4 tablespoons mayonnaise mixed with
    2 tablespoons mustard
4 tomato slices
iceberg lettuce leaves

Mix together the flour, cornmeal, Old Bay, and salt on a plate. Arrange near a shallow bowl containing the eggs. Dip each dried crab first in the egg, and then in the cornmeal mixture. Pat to evenly coat.

Pour the oil to a depth of ½ inch in a skillet large enough to hold 2 crabs. Heat 2 minutes over medium-high and add crabs, soft side up. Fry until golden brown and crisp, about 3 minutes per side. Drain on paper towels and repeat with second batch.

To make sandwiches, spread the rolls with the mustard/mayonnaise combination. Place a crab on each of the bottom halves. Top with tomato and lettuce, close, and slice to serve.

SERVES 4

"Blue crabmeat is as white as snow, as sweet as butter, and as dainty as a debutante."
　　　—*Steven Raichlen*

SOFTSHELL CRABS IN VEGETABLE BLACK BEAN SAUCE

This quick stir-fry is a bright, colorful one-skillet supper to serve over steamed rice. Prepared black bean sauce is available in Asian markets.

½ cup fish *or* chicken stock
1 tablespoon prepared black bean garlic sauce
1 tablespoon soy sauce
1 teaspoon sugar
4 softshell crabs, cleaned and patted dry
all-purpose *or* rice flour for dredging
salt and freshly ground pepper to taste
2 tablespoons peanut *or* vegetable oil
1 teaspoon minced ginger
1 teaspoon minced garlic
4 ounces snow peas, trimmed and julienned
4 ounces jicama, peeled and julienned
1 large carrot, trimmed and julienned
2 tablespoons butter

In a small bowl, mix together the fish stock, black bean sauce, soy sauce, and sugar. Set aside.

Lightly dredge the crabs in flour, patting off excess. Heat 1 tablespoon of the oil in a large nonstick skillet over medium-high heat. Cook the crabs about 2 minutes per side (be careful of splatters) and remove to a platter.

Add the remaining oil to the hot pan and briefly sauté the ginger and garlic. Add snow peas, jicama, and carrot, and stir-fry 2 to 3 minutes. Pour in the reserved black bean mixture and boil 2 minutes. Reduce heat to low and stir in the butter to thicken sauce. Return crabs to pan and toss just to evenly coat and heat through. Serve hot.

SERVES 4

CRAB DINNERS

BOILED CRABS
WITH CRAB BUTTER

If you are lucky enough to find live crabs, here is the easiest way to get them onto the table.

Place live crabs in the kitchen sink and run cold water over them for several minutes to remove dirt. Then fill the sink with cold water and ice cubes to keep the crabs happy. Fill your largest pot with water, add salt, cover, and bring to a boil.

Using tongs, pick up the crabs from the back and plunge them into the boiling water head first. Be prepared for a fight. Have a second imple-ment nearby (a spatula, second pair of tongs, or mallet) to encourage any cowards to get into the pot.

Cover the pot; cook Dungeness crabs about 8 minutes, or blue or rock crabs about 5, until they turn bright orange-red. Do not be concerned with legs or claws that break off; they will still be edi-ble. Remove crabs with tongs and set aside in a large colander to cool. (Blue crabs may be served whole, for the eaters to pull apart and suck at will. Don't forget the bibs.)

To serve larger crabs, wait until they are cool, and then twist off the triangular belly apron. Turn hard-shell side up, and pull off and discard the shell and any brown liquid. Remove and discard the spongy gills on either side and the tiny paddles from the front. Scoop out the orange crab "mustard" from the center and reserve.

With a heavy chef's knife, cut the body into quarters. Twist off the legs and claws, and crack each with a small hammer or a heavy rolling pin. Use a metal pick or lobster fork to pick out the meat, if desired. Store in the refrigerator.

CRAB BUTTER

A small Dungeness has about 1 tablespoon of luscious yellow-orange "mustard" in its sac. Blended with butter, it makes an extravagant dip for shellfish.

  4 tablespoons crab mustard *or* orange innards
  6 tablespoons butter
  salt to taste

Combine the crab mustard, butter, and salt in a small pot. Cook over low heat until butter is melted. Salt to taste and serve with hot or cold crab for dipping.

SERVES 4

"Extracting fish from a shell tends to be time-consuming, but shellfish eaters are, as a group, patient. In fact, the most pedantic among them...sometimes seem more interested in extracting crabmeat with finesse than in eating it."
        —Calvin Trillin

MARYLAND STEAMED CRABS

Eating Maryland-style crabs is a workout. They are meant to be scorching hot and spicy, pulled apart at the table, and sucked and picked upon with fervor. An outside space, preferably near a hose, is the best venue for such a feast. This authentic recipe was inspired by cookbook author and Baltimorean Steve Raichlen.

2 cups water
1 cup white vinegar
⅓ cup Old Bay seasoning
2 tablespoons coarse salt
2 tablespoons dry mustard
1 tablespoon cracked black pepper
2 to 3 teaspoons red chile flakes
12 live blue crabs

In a large pot with a steaming rack, combine the water and vinegar. In a small bowl, mix together the Old Bay, salt, mustard, pepper, and chile flakes.

Layer the crabs on the rack, sprinkling the spice mixture over each layer. Tightly cover, placing a weight on the lid to deter escapees. Boil over high heat until the crabs are bright red, about 20 minutes. Turn them out onto a newspaper-covered table, preferably outdoors, and dig in. Drawn butter and lemon are fitting accompaniments.

SERVES 2

To Eat a Blue Crab
Serve crabs with little hammers, nutcrackers, or sharp paring knives. Long, thin forks or picks are nice but not necessary. A bowl (or trash can) makes a good receptacle for shells. First, twist and pull off the legs and claws. Crack the claws to extract the meat, and suck on the tiny legs. As for the body, which is full of thin, white cartilage and delectable little crevices, first invert and pull off the V-shaped apron. Insert a paring knife beneath the top shell to lift and twist it off. Then scrape away the feathery gills and innards, break apart the body, and suck, pick, pull, or scrape out the best part.

PENNE WITH
FRESH TOMATOES AND CRAB

*This light, fresh pasta owes its luxuriousness to
the crab.*

2 tablespoons olive oil
3 large shallots, minced
¼ teaspoon red pepper flakes
4 plum tomatoes, chopped
1 cup fish stock *or* ½ cup clam juice and
    ½ cup water
¼ teaspoon crushed saffron threads (optional)
¾ pound flaked crabmeat
1 pound penne *or* spaghetti, cooked and drained
1 bunch chives, sliced
salt and freshly ground pepper to taste

Heat the oil in a large skillet over medium heat. Sauté the shallots with red pepper flakes until soft, about 5 minutes. Add the tomatoes and cook another 5 minutes. Pour in the fish stock and (optional) saffron. Bring to a boil and cook 8 to 10 minutes, until thickened. Stir in the crabmeat and cook 5 minutes to heat through.

Place the pasta in a serving bowl, add the sauce, and toss well. Sprinkle with chives and serve.

SERVES 4

America's best-selling crab is the blue crab from the East Coast. It is followed by the West Coast Dungeness, king from Alaska, and Florida stone crabs. The industry is centered in Louisiana, Florida, Alaska, California, Washington, and Oregon.

ASIAN CRAB NOODLES

Pan-fried noodles, enlivened with Thai spices and crabmeat, are an interesting switch on the usual pasta dinner.

8 ounces dried Chinese wheat noodles *or*
   angel hair pasta
peanut oil for coating
¼ cup fish *or* chicken stock
2 tablespoons Thai fish sauce *or* soy sauce
1 tablespoon brown sugar
1 tablespoon lime juice
1 egg
½ pound crabmeat, flaked
3 garlic cloves, minced
½-inch length ginger, peeled and grated
¼ cup chopped fresh cilantro for garnish

Cook the noodles in boiling salted water until soft. Drain, rinse with cold water, and transfer to a bowl. Pour on 1 or 2 tablespoons of oil and toss to evenly coat. Chill.

In a small bowl, mix together stock, fish or soy sauce, brown sugar, and lime juice and reserve. In another bowl, beat the egg and mix in crabmeat.

Heat a large skillet or wok over high heat. Lightly coat with oil. Add the crab-egg mixture and stir-fry about a minute. Push mixture to the pan's edges.

In the center, add the garlic and ginger, and stir-fry less than a minute. Add the noodles and stir-fry, combining all the ingredients, about 5 minutes. Pour in the reserved stock mixture and continue tossing and cooking 5 minutes longer to thoroughly heat and develop the flavors. Tip out onto a platter, garnish with cilantro, and serve hot or cold.

SERVES 2 TO 4

MARYLAND CRAB CAKES

For authentic Maryland flavor, purchase East Coast blue crabmeat, available pasteurized and frozen at fish markets.

5-inch length day-old baguette, crusts removed, cubed
¼ cup milk
1 egg
1 tablespoon mayonnaise
1 tablespoon Dijon mustard
1 teaspoon Worcestershire sauce
1 pound lump blue crabmeat, in chunks
2 tablespoons chopped fresh Italian parsley
1 teaspoon Old Bay seasoning
½ teaspoon salt
3 to 4 tablespoons butter
lemon wedges for garnish

Combine the bread cubes and milk in a bowl to evenly moisten.

In a large bowl, beat together egg, mayonnaise, mustard, and Worcestershire. Add the crabmeat, parsley, Old Bay, and salt and mix lightly just to combine. Gently press into 4 to 6 patties.

Heat the butter in a large skillet over medium-high heat. With a spatula, carefully slide the cakes into the pan and fry about 3 minutes per side, until golden and crisp. Serve with lemon wedges, mayonnaise, or your favorite dipping sauce.

SERVES 2 TO 4

The Annual Hard Crab Derby and Fair, held every Labor Day weekend since 1947 in Crisfield, Maryland, is the king of the crab festivals. The festivities include a race for the crabs, a crab-picking contest for the humans, and plenty of spiced, steamed crabs for the spectators.

THAI CRAB CAKES

Though our hearts belong to the original Maryland crab cakes, these spicy little cousins are a divine small meal.

½ cup rice vinegar
¼ cup brown sugar
2 tablespoons Thai fish sauce
4 teaspoons minced garlic
6 serrano *or* Thai chiles, stemmed, seeded, and minced
1 pound crabmeat
2 tablespoons chopped cilantro
2 tablespoons chopped scallion
2 teaspoons soy sauce
2 eggs, lightly beaten
⅔ cup dry bread crumbs
seasoned flour
vegetable oil
cilantro sprigs

In small saucepan, combine vinegar, sugar, 1 tablespoon fish sauce, 2 teaspoons garlic, and half of the chiles. Bring to a boil, reduce heat, and simmer 5 minutes. Transfer to a bowl and cool.

In another bowl, combine crab and the remaining fish sauce, garlic, and chiles. Add cilantro, scallion, soy sauce, eggs, and bread crumbs. Mix to blend thoroughly. Gently shape into flat cakes about 3 inches in diameter. Dip in flour to coat on both sides. Set on a baking sheet covered with waxed paper and chill at least 30 minutes.

Heat about 2 tablespoons oil over medium-high heat in a large skillet. Add crab cakes a few at a time, and cook until golden, about 5 minutes. Turn and cook about 5 minutes longer. Top with sauce and cilantro sprigs and serve immediately.

SERVES 6

RICH MAN'S FRIED RICE

Fried rice is a great way to stretch a few ingredients into a satisfying meal.

3 tablespoons peanut oil
½ pound crabmeat
1 (4-ounce) slice, about ¼ inch, honey-cured
   ham, cubed
2 eggs beaten with 1 teaspoon sesame oil
1 tablespoon minced garlic
2 teaspoons grated ginger
3 cups chilled, cooked white rice
salt and freshly ground pepper to taste
1 tablespoon soy sauce

Heat 1 tablespoon of the oil in a large skillet or wok over high heat. Stir-fry crabmeat and ham less than a minute. Transfer to a platter.

Pour in the eggs, swirl to make a thin pancake, and then quickly scramble. Transfer to the platter.

Heat the remaining oil in the pan over high heat. Stir-fry the garlic and ginger less than a minute. Add the rice, season with salt and pepper, and stir-fry until hot and coated with oil. Add the reserved crab, ham, and egg. Stir-fry a few minutes longer to heat through. Sprinkle with soy sauce and serve.

SERVES 4

QUICK CRAB RAVIOLI

These delicate ravioli are easy to make with store-bought wonton wrappers, available in the refrigerator case at the supermarket. For an elegant Italian meal, serve with "Tomato Butter Sauce;" for a quick Asian dinner, just use the dipping sauce.

1 pound lump crabmeat
1 large egg white
2 teaspoons rice vinegar
5 scallions, white and green, minced
grated zest of 1 lemon
1 teaspoon grated fresh ginger
about 28 wonton skins
cornstarch *or* flour for dusting

In a bowl, lightly combine the crabmeat, egg white, rice vinegar, scallions, lemon zest, and ginger. (The filling may be kept in the refrigerator up to 4 hours.)

To fill ravioli, arrange the wontons, a small bowl of cold water, and a tray dusted with cornstarch or flour on the work counter. Place a wonton on the counter and put a scant tablespoonful of filling in the center. With a finger dipped in the water, lightly moisten all 4 edges of wonton. Top with another wonton skin, pressing the dry and moist edges together to seal. Transfer to a tray and repeat until all ravioli are filled. (The tray can be kept in the refrigerator up to 6 hours before cooking.)

To cook, bring a large saucepan of salted water to a boil. Add the ravioli, a few at a time, and stir with slotted spoon to avoid sticking. When they rise to the top and are boiling rapidly, cook another 20 seconds. Remove with slotted spoon, shaking off water, and transfer to serving dishes. Top with "Tomato Butter Sauce" on page 76 or "Soy Scallion Dip" on page 77 and serve.

SERVES 4

TOMATO BUTTER SAUCE

4 tablespoons butter
2 tomatoes, peeled, seeded, and diced
2 tablespoons chopped fresh basil
salt and freshly ground pepper to taste

Combine the butter, tomatoes, and basil in a small pot. Season with salt and pepper and cook over low heat 3 minutes. Transfer to a blender and purée.

MAKES $^1/_2$ CUP

Stone crab, or Menippe mercenaria, is legendary for its thick, sweet claw meat and its Miami Beach following. The claws of this Florida native are always sold frozen. In fact, it is illegal to capture the whole stone crab. Fishermen catch these crabs in pots, twist off the larger of the two claws, and then toss the live crabs back in the water, where they grow a new claw, or retread, within the year. Stone crabs can be declawed three or four times in a lifetime. Stone crab claws are easy to recognize in the

SOY SCALLION DIP

3 tablespoons soy sauce
3 tablespoons rice vinegar
3 scallions, white and green, thinly sliced on the
    diagonal

Combine the ingredients in a small bowl.

MAKES $1/3$ CUP

market because of their wide shape and blackened tips.
The Miami landmark restaurant Joe's Stone Crab serves
them iced with a mustard dipping sauce. (The mixture of
one part honey mustard to two parts mayonnaise with
juice of one lemon is easy and delicious.) Allow at least
six juicy claws per guest, and have good, strong crackers
or hammers at the ready, since stone crab shells are quite
thick. In California, they are available frozen at fish
shops and Asian markets.

CRAB NORFOLK

This quick American classic is so rich, it is best served like a dip with crackers. It was created at the Snowden and Mason Restaurant in Norfolk, Virginia, in the 1920s.

6 tablespoons butter
1 pound lump blue crabmeat
3 tablespoons white wine *or* apple cider vinegar
4 dashes Tabasco
½ teaspoon Worcestershire sauce
freshly ground pepper to taste
½ cup chopped scallions, white and green

Melt the butter in a skillet over medium heat. Stir in the crabmeat, vinegar, Tabasco, Worcestershire, and pepper and cook just to heat through, about 3 minutes. Transfer to a serving dish, sprinkle with scallions, and serve with rice as an entrée or with crackers as an appetizer.

SERVES 4 TO 6

The blue crab, known as Callinectes sapidus, or "beautiful swimmer," is the most popular crab in America. Originally associated with the Chesapeake Bay in Maryland, blue crabs are now harvested all along the East Coast, from Cape Cod to Florida, and along the Gulf Coast, primarily in Louisiana. Because they are small—about 5 inches across—and yield only about 15-percent meat, blue crabs are the most work to pick. Either boil or steam and serve them whole, with plenty of napkins, or purchase pasteurized meat to use in crab cakes and other dishes. Live blue crabs are available all year round (on the East Coast), with summer the peak season. For a blue crab feast, allow 6 to 12 per guest, depending on the size of the crabs.

CRAB IMPERIAL

In this classic American dish, chunks of crabmeat are bathed in white sauce and then topped with a bit of cheese and crackers for crunch. Helene's husband, a native of Baltimore, inhaled all four servings.

3 cups low-fat milk
1 stick butter
½ cup all-purpose flour
½ teaspoon salt
¼ teaspoon pepper
pinch of cayenne and paprika
2 tablespoons lemon juice
1 pound lump blue crabmeat
1 red bell pepper, seeded and diced
¾ cup shredded cheddar cheese
¾ cup crushed salty crackers

Preheat oven to 350 degrees F and coat an
8- or 9-inch casserole with butter.

To make the white sauce, bring the milk nearly
to a boil in a small pot and remove from heat. In
another heavy saucepan, melt the butter over
low heat. Whisk in the flour and continue whisking until pale gold, about 5 minutes. Gradually
whisk in the warm milk and cook until mixture
comes back to a boil, whisking constantly.
Remove from heat, whisk in salt, pepper,
cayenne, and paprika and transfer to large bowl.
Cool slightly. Add lemon juice, crabmeat, and
bell pepper and mix well.

Spoon the mixture into the coated casserole,
spreading to make an even layer. Toss together
the cheese and crumbs and sprinkle over the top.
Bake 30 to 40 minutes, until golden and bubbly.
Serve hot.

SERVES 4

CRAB IN BROTH
WITH GARLIC AND SPINACH

We like to serve crab in the shell in a brothy dish like this so the shells catch the fragrant juices. Serve with a warm, crusty sourdough bread for soaking up stray broth.

¼ cup olive oil
3 tablespoons minced garlic
1 onion, chopped
1 celery rib, minced
2 tomatoes, seeded and chopped
¼ teaspoon red pepper flakes
salt and freshly ground pepper to taste
3 cups fish stock
1 (6-ounce) package baby spinach
2 pounds cooked, cleaned Dungeness crab in
   the shell, quartered and cracked

Heat the oil in a large heavy pot over medium-high heat. Sauté the garlic, onion, and celery 5 minutes. Add tomatoes, red pepper flakes, salt, and pepper and cook another 5 minutes.

Pour in the stock and bring to a boil for 3 minutes. Stir in the spinach and cook until wilted. Stir in the crab and cook another minute or two, just to heat through. Ladle into shallow bowls and serve hot.

SERVES 4

"There are two schools of thought about eating cracked crab. There are those who eat the crab meat as fast as the shells are removed. Others dig out all of the meat from their entire portion, to eat at leisure when the work is done. Adherents of the former procedure are invariably scornful of those in the latter category."
—Helen Evans Brown

FILLET OF SOLE
IN CRAB-CREAM SAUCE

This creamy saffron crab sauce served with delicate sole makes a big impression at less cost than a whole crab dinner. With steamed greens, rice, and a good bottle of wine, you'll have an elegant dinner party menu.

¼ cup minced scallions
½ teaspoon minced garlic
½ cup dry white wine
¾ cup fish stock
large pinch of saffron
1 cup heavy cream
4 ounces flaked crabmeat
½ teaspoon Dijon mustard
salt and freshly ground pepper to taste
4 (5-ounce) sole fillets
2 tablespoons butter

Combine the scallions, garlic, and white wine in a medium saucepan and bring to a boil over high heat. Reduce until 2 tablespoons of liquid remain. Pour in the fish stock and saffron and boil until about ¼ cup of liquid remains. Add the cream and boil about 4 minutes, until thickened to taste. Reduce the heat to low. Stir in crabmeat and mustard and cook just to heat through. Adjust seasonings with salt and pepper and reserve.

Season the fish all over with salt and pepper. Melt the butter in a nonstick pan over medium-high heat. Cook the fish about 2 minutes per side. Place fish on serving plates, spoon on the sauce, and serve.

SERVES 4

CHAMPAGNE AND CRAB RISOTTO

As wonderful as champagne may sound, white wine will do just fine in this lovely Italian rice dish.

4 tablespoons butter
4 shallots, diced
1 garlic clove, minced
2 cups Arborio rice
½ cup flat champagne *or* white wine
4 cups fish stock *or* 2 cups clam juice and
    2 cups water, warmed
pinch of saffron
1 pound flaked crabmeat
¼ cup chopped fresh Italian parsley
salt and freshly ground pepper to taste

Melt 2 tablespoons of the butter in a heavy medium saucepan over medium heat. Sauté the shallots and garlic until soft. Stir in the rice and cook to evenly coat. Pour in the champagne or wine and cook until the liquid is absorbed.

Add the saffron to the warm stock and ladle 1 cup of stock into the rice, stirring continuously over moderate heat. Continue adding warm broth, ½ cup at a time, stirring constantly, until the liquid is absorbed and the rice is done but *al dente* in the center. Reduce heat to very low and stir in crabmeat, parsley, and remaining butter. Season with salt and pepper, remove from heat, and let sit 10 minutes. Serve hot.

SERVES 6

"Probably the best place to eat stone crab would be the bath tub. The fingers are used in toying with them. Some high-toned folks use these dinky little oyster forks, but the fingers are far speedier and more efficient."
    —*Damon Runyon*

CRAB CURRY

*This sweet and fiery dish has the fragrant fruitiness
of a typical Thai curry.*

2 tablespoons vegetable oil
1 large onion, cut in thin wedges
1 green bell pepper, stemmed, seeded,
    and julienned
1 tablespoon minced garlic
1 tablespoon minced ginger
1 serrano *or* Thai chile, stemmed, seeded,
    and minced
2 tablespoons curry powder
1 (28-ounce) can diced tomatoes
¾ cup unsweetened coconut milk
1½ pounds crabmeat
hot cooked basmati rice
cilantro leaves

Heat oil in a large heavy pot over medium-high heat. Add onion, bell pepper, garlic, ginger, and chile. Cook, stirring frequently, until tender, about 5 minutes. Stir in curry powder and cook 1 minute longer. Stir in tomatoes with their liquid. Bring to a boil, reduce heat, and simmer 10 minutes. Whisk in coconut milk and simmer 10 minutes longer, stirring occasionally. Stir in crabmeat and cook just until heated through, about 3 minutes. Serve over rice and garnish with cilantro.

SERVES 6

GARLIC STEAMED CRAB

If you love crabs, chances are that garlic is never far from your mind when you dream about eating your favorite crustacean.

½ stick butter
2 tablespoons minced garlic
2 whole cleaned and cooked Dungeness crabs, about 4 pounds, cracked
2 cups dry white wine
1 cup peeled, seeded, and diced tomatoes
1 tablespoon lemon juice
1 teaspoon grated lemon zest
¼ cup chopped fresh Italian parsley
lemon wedges
1 hot baguette, sliced

Melt butter in a large heavy skillet over medium heat. Add garlic and sauté about 30 seconds. Add crabs and toss to coat. Pour in wine and bring to a boil. Stir in tomatoes, lemon juice, zest, and parsley. Reduce heat, cover, and simmer 3 minutes.

Serve with lemon wedges and pass baguette slices for sopping up sauce.

SERVES 6

To Catch a Crab

The best time to catch crabs is neither high nor low tide, but when currents are relatively still so the scent of bait can be followed. A crab's favorite foods, according to fishermen, or watermen (never "crabbers"— which is considered a derogatory term), are smaller crabs, clams, squid, mussels, and small fish. The bait is placed in a jar with holes that allow the aroma to escape, and the jar goes inside a crab pot or trap.

To hold a live crab, first stop it from moving by stepping on the shell with your foot. Then grasp it from the back, with your fingers in the center of the top shell and a thumb underneath. If you do get pinched, resist flinging it off, since it may only shed a claw. Calmly wait for the crab to loosen its grip; then say thank you, and retreat.

CRAB ENCHILADAS VERDE

Tart green tomatillos and earthy tortillas are a good foil for rich crabmeat.

   vegetable oil
   1 onion, chopped
   3 garlic cloves, minced
   1 (7-ounce) can diced green chiles
   2 (12-ounce) cans tomatillos, drained
   ½ cup chopped cilantro
   12 corn tortillas
   1½ pounds crabmeat
   ¾ cup sliced scallions
   2 cups crumbled cotija cheese *or* shredded
      Monterey Jack cheese
   1 cup sour cream

Heat 3 tablespoons of oil in a skillet over medium-high heat. Add onion and sauté until soft. Add garlic and sauté 30 seconds longer. Stir in green chiles, tomatillos, and cilantro. Bring to a boil, reduce heat, and simmer 15 minutes. Set aside to cool.

In another skillet, heat ¼ cup oil over medium heat. Add tortillas, one at a time, and fry just until softened. Drain on paper towels.

Preheat oven to 350 degrees F.

Transfer tomatillo mixture to blender and process until a chunky sauce is formed. Spoon 1 cup sauce onto bottom of a 13 x 9-inch baking dish.

In bowl, combine crabmeat, 1 cup tomatillo sauce, all but ¼ cup scallions, and 1½ cups cheese. Divide mixture evenly onto centers of tortillas, roll into cylinders, and arrange in a single layer in a prepared baking dish. Spoon remaining sauce evenly over enchiladas. Cover with foil and bake 10 minutes, then sprinkle with remaining cheese and dollop with sour cream. Bake, uncovered, 10 minutes longer. Sprinkle with remaining green onions and serve hot.

SERVES 6

CRAB AND GREENS IN BLACK BEAN GARLIC SAUCE

Fermented black beans are one of the classic Chinese accompaniments to crab.

¼ cup vegetable oil
2 tablespoons minced garlic
2 tablespoons minced fresh ginger
8 cups chopped Chinese broccoli, baby bok choy,
    or Chinese cabbage
¼ cup prepared black bean garlic sauce
¼ cup rice wine
2 tablespoons soy sauce
1 tablespoon sugar
1½ pounds king crab legs, cooked, thawed,
    and cracked
1 tablespoon cornstarch
2 tablespoons water

Heat oil in wok over high heat. Add garlic and ginger and stir-fry 30 seconds. Add broccoli and stir-fry just until wilted, about 3 minutes. Stir in black bean sauce, rice wine, soy sauce, and sugar. Lay crab legs over mixture, reduce heat, cover, and simmer 3 minutes.

Meanwhile, mix together cornstarch and water. Remove crab legs and reserve on platter. Stir cornstarch mixture into pan, raise heat, and stir until liquid is thickened and clear. Return crab legs to wok and stir to evenly coat. Serve crab legs over broccoli.

SERVES 4

Crabs are among the most prized ingredients in Chinese cuisine—with the female's eggs considered a great delicacy. Crabs are stocked live in better restaurants, and if they are in season anywhere, Chinese markets are bound to have them (at a good price) both live in tanks and frozen. According to Chinese mythology, the crab lost its voice and acquired its homely shape as a punishment for tattling. An angry cow stamped on the crab for telling a farmer that the cow was eating his rice.

CONVERSIONS

LIQUID
  1 Tbsp = 15 ml
  1/2 cup = 4 fl oz = 125 ml
  1 cup = 8 fl oz = 250 ml
DRY
  1/4 cup = 4 Tbsp = 2 oz = 60 g
  1 cup = 1/2 pound = 8 oz = 250 g
FLOUR
  1/2 cup = 60 g
  1 cup = 4 oz = 125 g
TEMPERATURE
  400° F = 200° C = gas mark 6
  375° F = 190° C = gas mark 5
  350° F = 175° C = gas mark 4
MISCELLANEOUS
  2 Tbsp butter = 1 oz = 30 g
  1 inch = 2.5 cm
  all-purpose flour = plain flour
  sugar = caster sugar